Fun with frie...

JUMBO Coloring & Activity Book

BENDON™

©2006
Bendon Publishing International, Inc.
Ashland, OH 44805
www.bendonpub.com

SESAME STREET

Follow the footsteps to take Grover to see his friends.

How many circles can you find in this picture?

Fun at the carnival!

Decorate the carousel horse.

Find the picture of Big Bird that is different.

First place finish in the carnival art show!

Decorate this bike for the big carnival parade!

Help Big Bird catch up to Elmo.

Draw lines to connect the matching balloons.

Draw a picture of your best friend.

Circle the things Elmo would take on a picnic with Zoe.

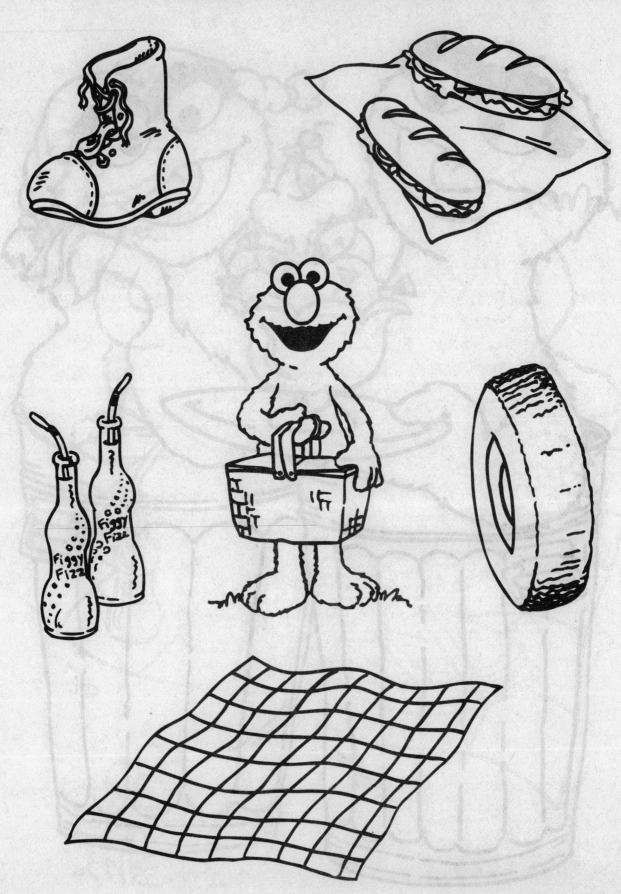

What food would you bring on a picnic lunch? Draw it.

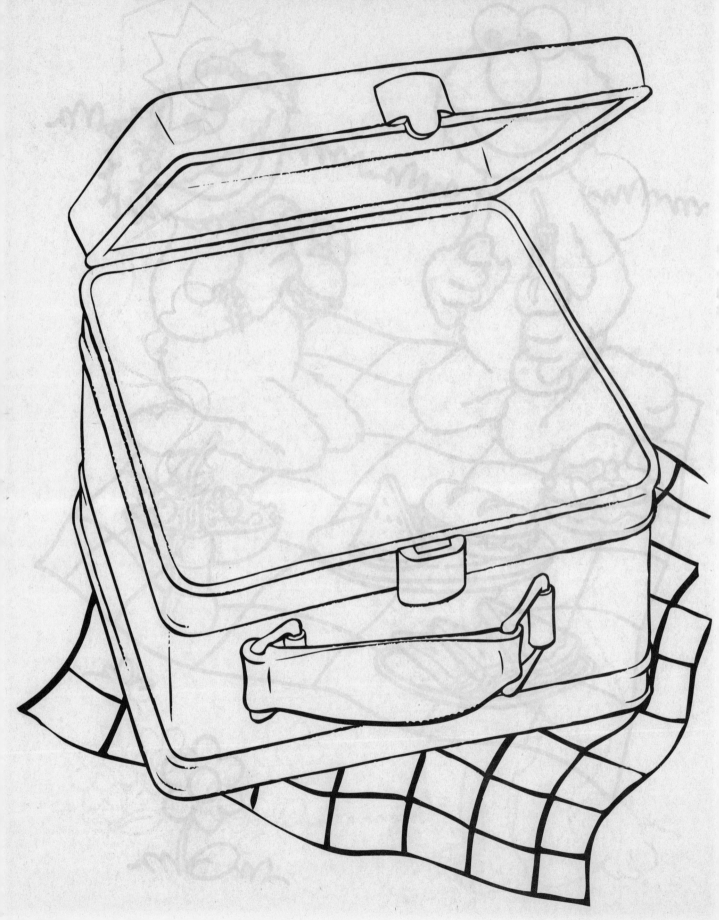

Connect the dots to see what Elmo is doing.

9 •

10 •

8 •

7 • • 11

6 • • 12

5 • • 13

3 • 4 •

2 • • 14

• 15

Start 1 •

What does Big Bird see in the clouds?

Fun with animal friends!

Petting
Farm

Help the Count connect the numbers. Count the bats.

Draw a picture of your favorite animal friend.

Draw a line from Elmo to the fish that is his pet.

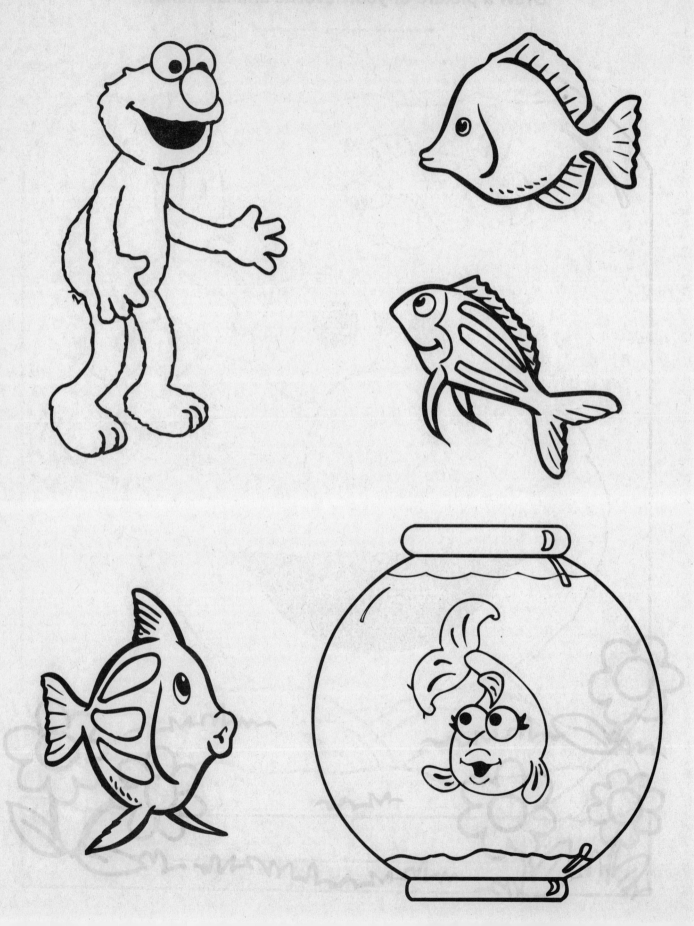

I , Grover, am your friend!

Me your friend, too!

It's fun to share with friends!

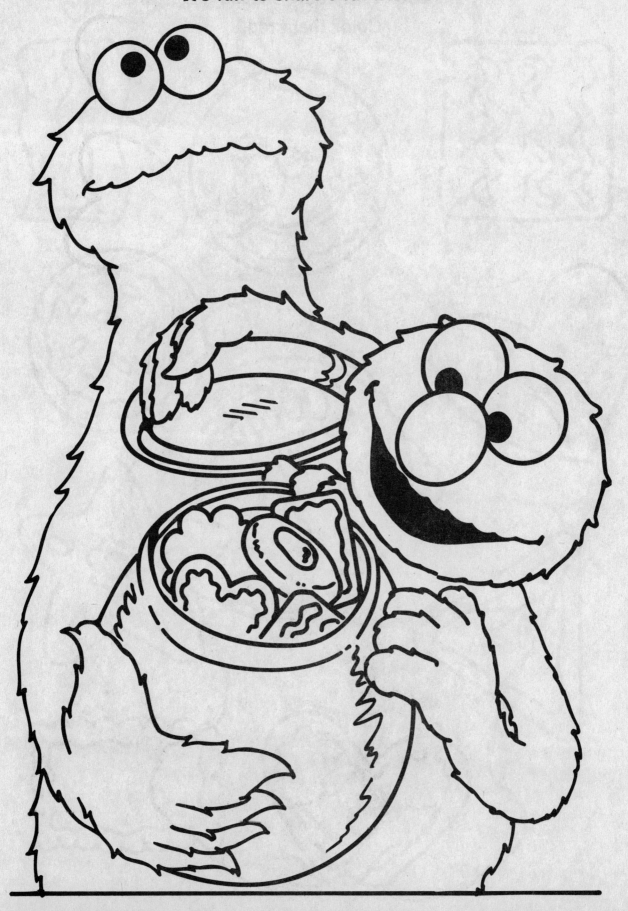

Color them red.

How many cookies are in this jar? Count them to find out.

Sing a song with a friend!

Play sports with a friend!

Take Elmo to the net.

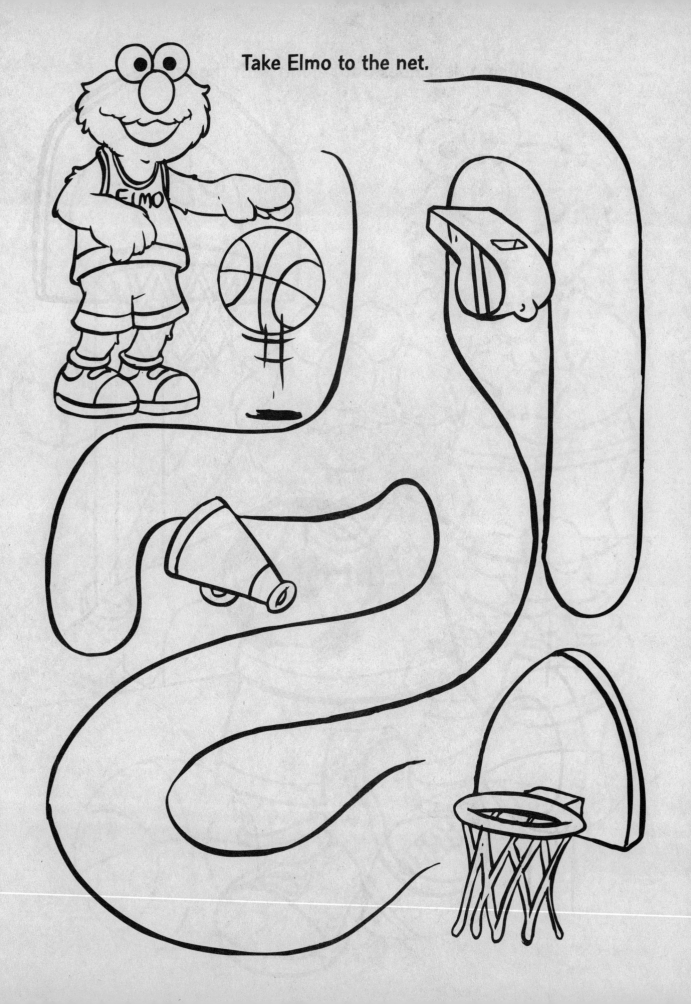

Which object does not belong with the others?

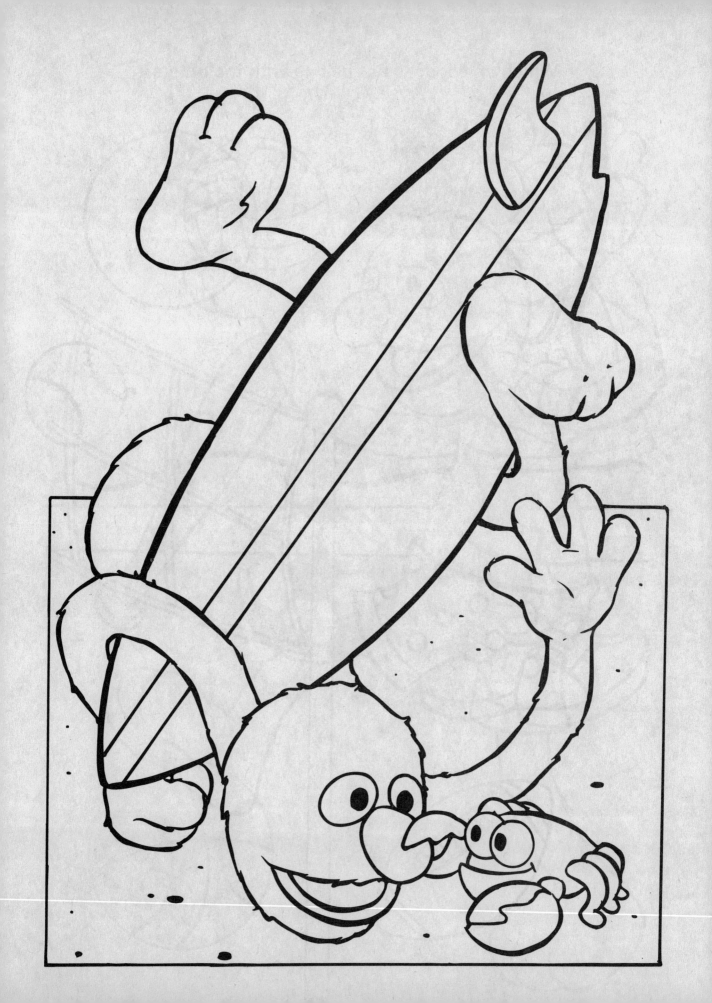

Connect the dots.

Find a way to the beach.

Finish

Start

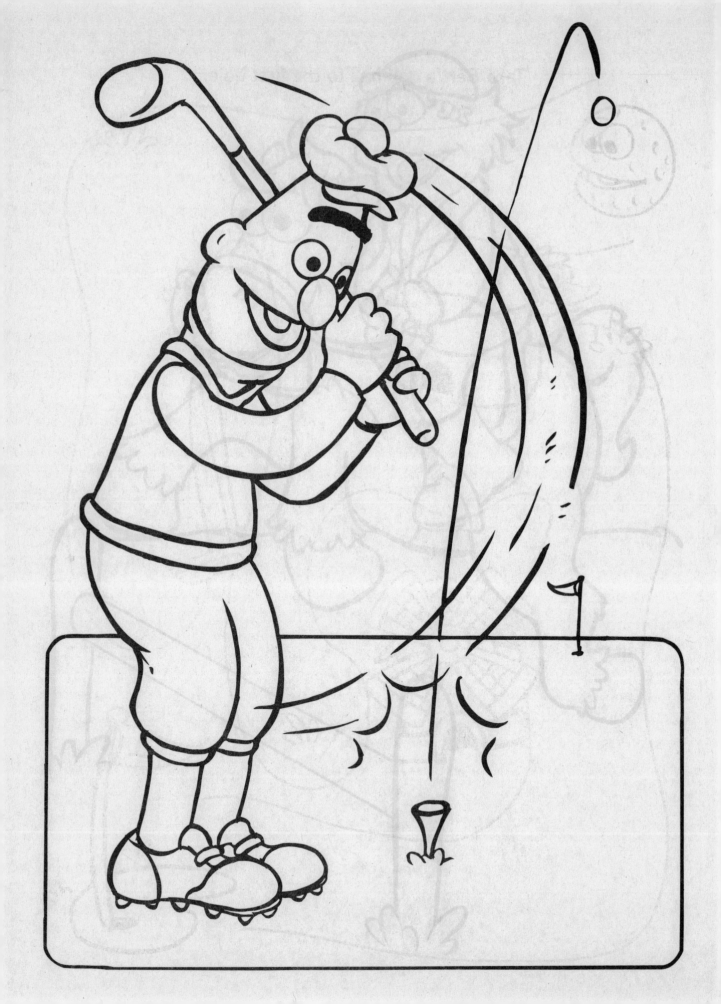

Take Bert's golf ball to the first hole.

Which picture of Bert is different?

Take Bert to the finish line!

FINISH

Who will win the race?

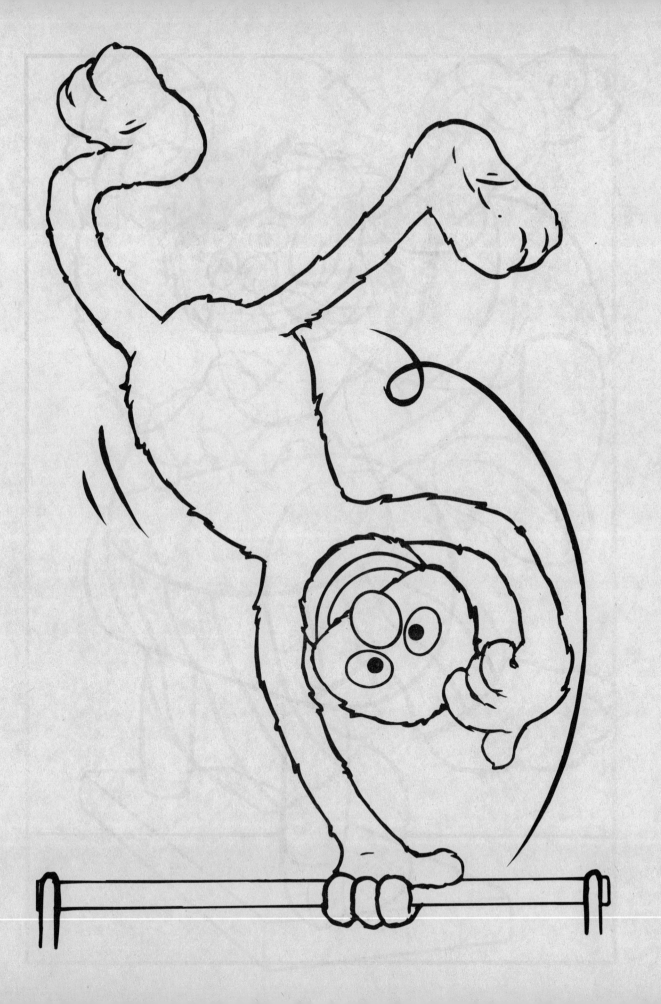

Elmo has friends all over the world
like Zeliboba in Russia, Nimnim in Egypt,
Kami in South Africa, Hu Hu Zhu in China,
and Ieniemienie in The Netherlands.

Thank you!